Satisfaction
GUARANTEED

Satisfaction GUARANTEED

236 IDEAS TO MAKE YOUR
CUSTOMERS FEEL LIKE
A MILLION DOLLARS

BYRD BAGGETT

INSIGNIS, CORP.

Nashville, Tennessee

Published in Nashville, Tennessee, by Rutledge Hill Press,
211 Seventh Avenue North, Nashville, Tennessee 37219.

Typography by D&T/Bailey Typesetting,
Nashville, Tennessee
Design by Bruce Gore, Gore Studio

Library of Congress Cataloging-in-Publication Data

Baggett, Byrd.
    Satisfaction guaranteed : 236 ideas to make your
customers feel like a million dollars / Byrd Baggett.
        p.   cm.
    ISBN 1-55853-214-5
    1. Customer service — Quotations, maxims, etc.
    I. Title.
HF5415.5.B33 1994
658.8'12 — dc20   94-2500
                                                         CIP

Printed in the United States of America
2 3 4 5 6 7 8 — 99 98 97 96

With thanks to

Jeanne, my wonderful wife,
whose faith continues to bless me

Ashley, Amy, and Austin,
my three wonderful children

Byrd Baggett, Jr., my father,
for his strong belief in me

The many loving and supportive friends
who have encouraged and supported me

Introduction

IF YOU'VE EVER LOST a customer, I wrote this book for you.

For twenty-one years I have been in the business of satisfying customers. During this time I have pounded the streets, managed sales staffs, and run my own business. I have seen both success and failure up close and have studied each carefully, and I have learned that the key to success — for individuals and for businesses — is satisfied customers. This is true whether a company sells groceries, cleans floors, or handles stock transactions. Satisfied customers are repeat customers.

I am not the first person to notice this connection. Indeed, in some circles it has become almost a truism. Unfortunately, however, while there is much talk about customer service, so little is actually delivered that many people are startled when a business treats them well.

Satisfied customers don't just happen. They are the result of truly *believing* that happy customers are the crucial ingredient of success and that their interests must come first.

It is important for your customers to know that you want them to be completely satisfied and will settle for nothing less. If you do not take good care of them, they will take their business to one of your competitors who will. If you are unwilling to improve in this area, there really is no point in looking for new customers — you probably will lose them, too.

If you read my first book, *The Book of Excellence,* you will remember that I learned the habits of successful selling by observing the best in the field. The same is true of customer service. The habits contained in this book are used constantly by the top service organizations in America, which is why they are among the country's most successful companies. These companies focus on pleasing their customers, and if you cultivate the same habits, you will have satisfied customers.

I believe passionately that it is not enough today to be just a good salesperson, secretary, or manager. We must strive to be the best at what we do. We must remember that we are only one bad experience away from losing any customer. That is why providing excellent service is so important.

As was the case in *The Book of Excellence,* there are no page numbers here, so start and end wherever you want. Whether you are someone who wants to do the best job possible or are responsible for managing the work of hundreds of employees, I believe that *Satisfaction Guaranteed* will remind you of what it takes to be successful in today's business environment.

— Byrd Baggett

Satisfaction
GUARANTEED

Do what you said
you were going to do, when
you said you were going to
do it, and how you said you
were going to do it.

Listen twice as much
as you talk.

Never argue with a customer who wants a refund or an exchange.

How many customers did you lose last year due to poor customer service?

Customer service is either good or bad. There is no in-between.

If you provide only 99 percent satisfaction, a million transactions mean ten thousand unhappy customers.

Offer your customers at least one service they cannot get anywhere else.

Once you lose customers to bad customer service, it is almost impossible to get them back.

Answer the phone by
the third ring.

Don't be afraid to lose
money to satisfy a customer.
Short-term losses can equal
long-term gains.

Response time
should be measured in
minutes, not hours.

If management doesn't
care about customer service,
employees won't either.

Don't accept mediocrity!

If your departments don't communicate effectively with each other, you can be sure they aren't communicating with your customers either.

Customers want to feel
important.

Study companies with
impressive service reputations,
such as L. L. Bean or
Federal Express.

You can increase sales by 30 percent by providing excellent customer service to your existing accounts.

Make sure your voice mail is not voice jail.

Never compete with
your customers.

Never put your customers
on hold without their
consent.

A negative attitude cancels out all positive skills.

It's easier to get customers than it is to keep them.

Toll-free customer service lines should not be a substitute for personal contact.

Develop ways to measure your level of customer service.

If possible, return all phone calls within one hour.

Remember, little things make a big difference.

This year improve your performance in at least three areas to serve your customers better.

Hire nice people.

Tell your customers how much you appreciate them. Then show them.

Underpromise. Overperform.

Never tell a customer,
"That's not my job!"

Customers communicate
with their wallets.

Empower all employees to
serve your customers.

Never be too busy
to follow up on
your customers' requests.

Never argue
with a customer.

Management needs
to spend time listening
to customers.

The best vehicle to develop increased sales is a first-rate customer service program.

Follow up, follow up, follow up.

Conduct feedback sessions
with major customers every
six months.

Take action immediately
when you hear of a customer
service problem.

No employee is exempt
from serving your customers.

Always tell the truth.

Read at least one biography
or autobiography of a successful
business leader this year.

Customers will buy
from you if they like you.
The reverse is also true.

Never, ever, forget
the customer.

Consult customers
before introducing new
products or services.

Excellent customer service equals long-term success.

Ask your customers how you're doing. Theirs are the only answers that matter.

Terminate employees with bad attitudes.

Be as interested in the appetizers as you are the entrées. (Customers won't give large orders if you can't handle small ones.)

Indifference is deadly.

Give the customer service department complete responsibility and authority to make immediate decisions.

Never forget the basics.

A customer should never have to talk to more than two people for assistance: the receptionist and a customer service representative.

Customers should "hear" your smile over the phone.

Share customer service feedback with your employees on a regular basis.

Your corporate culture
should be built around
customer service excellence,
not products or service.

Customer service is much
more than a slogan.

Emulate companies with
excellent customer service
reputations.

Encourage those who
communicate with customers
by phone to meet them
personally.

People buy from people,
not machines.

Don't waste your time
trying to change employees
who have bad attitudes. Hire
people with good attitudes.

Use the mystery shopper
audit system.

Be honest.
Would you buy
from your company?

Customers will pay more
for excellent service.

A customer should
never have to search
for help.

Hold meetings in
which your customers explain
what they expect from
their suppliers.

Lower prices do not justify
poor customer service.

A positive image is
very important.

M ay I help you?"
(with a smile) is still
in vogue.

Old-fashioned customer
service still works.

Customers should expect
consistent quality and never
have to settle for mediocrity.

If you promise the moon,
be able to deliver it.

Small companies have an
advantage in maintaining a
philosophy of customer
service excellence.

Your first chance
may be your last.

Even one employee
who fails to buy into your
customer service program
will hurt the results.

Never say,
"I don't know." It is your
responsibility to know.

Customers should never
be made to feel they are
bothering you by expecting
excellent service.

If customers don't receive 100 percent satisfaction, they should not have to pay full price.

Reward your employees for excellent customer service.

At the end of the day, ask yourself, "Are all of my customers happy?"

Make sure all departments work together in pleasing your customers.

Customer service programs aren't expensive to implement.

If you want your business to grow, do the best job of serving customers in your industry.

Satisfaction guaranteed
or your money back"
was once the benchmark of
one of the best service
companies in America.

Listen, listen, listen.

The customer's perception
of the situation *is* reality.

&

Rapport is not
developed over the telephone.
Face-to-face interaction builds
long-term business
relationships.

Accept the challenge of satisfying the most difficult customers.

Poor customer service is the root of the problems of most companies.

Make sure your support
staff feels as important as
your sales staff.

The receptionist should not
put customers on hold.

Let common sense prevail.

Prior to making decisions, put yourself in your customers' shoes.

Customer service
should be fun.

Customer service
never goes out of style.

Without attention to
excellent customer service,
even a good marketing
plan will fail.

Are you becoming
complacent?

When you provide good service, your customers are the first to benefit.

Each day you either get better or worse. The choice is yours.

Send your customers
plants or flowers on special
occasions.

If you are doing the same
things this year that you did
last year, you're probably
losing ground.

Break bread with
your customers.

Expect excellence from
yourself and from others.

If you want
success, be serious about
your business.

A customer's opinion
is formed after the first
transaction.

Customers hate
to hear, "I'm sorry, but
they're in a meeting."

Keep customer service
surveys brief, and pay careful
attention to them.

Write it down.
Don't rely on your memory.

❦

Have someone available
to handle customer service
calls during all hours of
the business day.

If you follow up,
you'll stand out from
the crowd.

Customer service requires
a twenty-four-hour-a-day,
seven-days-a-week
commitment.

Don't just talk about it.
Do it!

Do your customers feel
that you truly appreciate their
business? Ask them.

You need your customers
more than they need you.

The customer service
budget is as important
as the advertising budget.

Don't focus on
developing new business until
you can effectively service
your existing customers.

❦

If you take
your customers for granted,
you'll lose them.

Set high customer service
goals. Monitor and modify
them constantly.

Never think you and your
company are more important
than your customers.

Remember,
customers have choices.

Use a beeper so that
the office can notify you of
a customer's emergency.

Don't talk down to
your customers.

The receptionist is one
of the most important
customer service persons in
your organization.

Don't expect your customers to tell you they're unhappy with your level of service.

Customers like positive people.

Show your customers
how good you are.
Don't tell them.

Spend as much time
on customer service training
as you do on sales training.

Genuinely care about
your customers.

If you don't like people,
you shouldn't be in business.

Sales gets customers;
service keeps them.

C

Have a toll-free
customer service line,
preferably open twenty-four
hours a day.

Make all your customers feel as if they're the most important.

Don't bother customers during their busy times.

Customer service is
everyone's job.

Do your competitors
offer superior customer
service? Match them or
get ready to be second best.

When you make a mistake, correct it immediately.

Make sure customer service opinion surveys have prepaid postage. Customers should not have to pay to give you their opinions.

Never have customers wait for employees who are on personal calls.

Don't get so hung up on administrivia that you ignore the customer.

Know what happens once your company receives a complaint.

Consistently share articles and books on customer service with your staff.

Don't be too proud to say,
"I'm sorry!"

Talking about customer
service is not the same as
providing it.

Handle complaints
promptly.

Evaluate what you're
doing right, as well as what
you're doing wrong.

Ask customers what they want. Then deliver.

Delegate decision-making ability; minimize the need for approvals.

Exceed your customers'
expectations.

Testimonials about
excellent service are the most
effective advertisements.

Communicate, communicate, communicate.

You will never be the best if your customer service is less than exceptional.

What happens to the information your customer service reps collect?

Happy customers tell few; unhappy customers tell many.

Customers want solutions,
not excuses.

Do the simple things in an
exceptional way.

Don't let prosperity cloud your objectivity about how customers see you.

Satisfied customers equal profits.

Minimize the paperwork
required to solve your
customers' problems.

Customer satisfaction
is an art.

Well-treated employees
treat customers well.

All employees should
either serve your customers
or assist those who do.

Outhustle your
competition.

No matter how large your
company, treat customers as if
your survival depends on
them. It does.

Get to know your customers on a first-name basis.

If you have high customer turnover, you're doing a poor job of serving your customers.

If your company isn't growing, it could be the result of poor-to-mediocre customer service.

Be calm when dealing with problems.

Never justify a problem.
Fix it instead.

Establish a minimum
response goal, and then
live by it.

There is a wealth of opportunity for those who please customers.

For a business to be successful, management must communicate the company's mission to all employees.

Don't judge a book
by its cover. Small customers
become big customers.

View customers as people,
not statistics.

Employees will
follow your lead,
good or bad.

Whenever possible,
do business with your
customers.

Warranties and guarantees should be unconditional.

Make sure you can service what you sell prior to taking it to the marketplace.

Poor service can make a
good product fail.

Continually seek
ways to improve your
customer service.

Bureaucracy and customer service are mutually exclusive.

Customer service should be the top priority in your company, from the bottom to the top.

Some of the greatest customer service ideas come from the least likely sources.

Reward employees who excel at customer service.

Customers should
have direct access to
top management.

If you are first in customer
service, you can ultimately be
first in sales.

A warranty is only as good
as you make it.

If you give bad service,
customers will leave you
without uttering a word.

Customers hate to hear,
"Can't it wait until Monday?"

Customers love to hear,
"What can I do to help you?"

Service is the highest value your customers are looking for.

If you substituted a customer appreciation banquet for the annual sales meeting, the results would be staggering.

Be creative and unconventional when solving your customers' problems.

Compensate your staff as much for keeping customers as you do for getting them.

Toll-free customer service
lines should be
adequately staffed.

Your customer service
standards should be
well defined.

Be thankful for customers
who complain. You still have
the opportunity to make
them happy.

Many customers will
never call you back after
a bad experience.

If you don't take care of your customers, your competitors will.

If you're having a bad day, don't let your customers "feel" it!

Develop a comprehensive
customer service training
program.

Customers hate to wait.

Customers despise
incompetence.

Management must practice
what it preaches.

If you advertise it,
you better have it.

Develop a customer
service mission statement.
Communicate it and live it!

Remember,
customers talk.

You can never train your
staff too much.

Develop ways
to make your customers
more profitable.

Ask your employees for
input on how to better serve
your customers. Their
feedback will surprise you.

Don't expand too quickly.

Never put your employees on the firing line without proper training.

Never compromise quality
for a lower price.

Be sure that
employees know and
understand company policies
and service contracts.

Hire a good mix of maturity and youth.

Occasionally have an employee or family member order from your competitors so you can know how well they serve their customers.

Reward customers for
referring new clients to you.

You can learn a lot about
how to improve customer
service when you work out
problems with your
own vendors.

Fill all orders before the
promised deadline.

Educate customers on
the best ways to use your
products and services.

Service your own products;
free of charge is best.

If you make an error,
try to correct it and notify
your customer before he or
she notices it.

Learn from your
mistakes.

When you are offering
a special price on an item,
refund the difference to anyone
who inadvertently paid
full price.

Always remember that
no one knows your client's
business better than
he or she does.

Include your customers
in your planning. You will
be surprised at how much
you learn.

If you want honest answers from your employees and customers, keep their responses in strict confidence.

Pay attention to the future. Anticipate the changing needs of your customers.

Stay in touch with your customers to be certain they are happy with your products and services.

Don't become so focused on new ideas and new customers that you forget the ideas and people who got you where you are.

Correct weaknesses
before they become
serious problems.

The only way to beat
your competition consistently
is to outservice them.

Say "Thank you" a lot.

The only goal for customer
service is 100 percent
customer satisfaction.

Excellence is not optional—
for you or your customer.

The customer is
always right.